Profiles in Faith

Profiles in Faith

A STUDY OF PEOPLE IN THE GOSPELS

DARREN CUSHMAN WOOD

North United Methodist Church • Indianapolis, IN

ISBN 978-1-7327761-9-7 (epub)

ISBN 979-8-9882332-0-6 (paperback)

The cover art comes from a small portion of one of the many beautiful banners throughout North United Methodist Church created by the late Doris Douglas, a long-time member, and other artists.

Contents

Introduction

They are called "driveway moments." They are stories you hear on the radio that are so compelling you have to sit in your car in the driveway to hear how they end.

The four stories featured in this study are New Testament "driveway moments." They are the profiles of people like you and me who struggled and grew in their faith. Each one of these stories features a key statement (set off in **bold** print) that expresses their trust and gives insight for the development of our faith.

Through the Spirit we are invited to enter their stories. When we identify with them, we can discover how the Spirit is at work in our own story. God has always been a part of your life, whether you realized it or not. The same Spirit who was at work in their lives has been shaping your life.

When you read the scripture passages, use "The Guided Reading of Scripture" at the back. It will help you explore the connections between you and the biblical characters and discover the Spirit through scripture. The notes at the end of each session will give you background information to help you understand the context of the scripture passages.

All scripture is taken from the New Revised Standard Version of the Bible, copyright 1989 by the Division of Christian

Education of the National Council of the Churches of Christ in the USA.

It is my prayer that you will have a "driveway moment" as you experience the Spirit of God through the reading of scripture and sharing your stories with one another.

SCRIPTURE MEDITATION

This process of guided reading is designed to help you enter the story of scripture. It is a playful and prayerful meditation – playful because you will use your imagination, and prayerful because the Spirit will use your imagination to illuminate the story. Use this process for reading the featured Bible story for each session.

1. Begin with a prayer for illumination: *Living God, open our hearts and minds that we may discover your truth, follow your way, and find your peace. Amen.*

2. Center yourself and then begin to read the passage (silently or aloud). As you read, imagine yourself in the story. Pause after every two or three verses and use your imagination to meditate on the following:

- Imagine the physical setting – Where you are, what time of day, the weather. What do you see, smell, hear, feel?
- Imagine the social setting – Who is there? What do they look like? What are they doing? What is their attitude and relationships?
- Imagine your name in place of the main character's name – How does it sound for the other characters to speak (or ignore) you? How does it feel for you to

speak the words of your character? How does it feel for Jesus to speak to you in the story?

3. End with a moment of silence to let the Spirit settle your thoughts and instill the insights you need to hear.

4. Throughout the day, reflect on the key verse, which is highlighted in bold.

1. Martha's Story – From Despair to Hope

INTRODUCTION

In her landmark study, "On Death and Dying," Elisabeth Kübler-Ross outlines the stages of grief and dying for the patient and the family: denial and isolation, anger, bargaining, depression, and acceptance. Death and other major crises challenge our faith.

In this session's story, we learn that Mary and Martha's brother, Lazarus, has recently died, and we see Martha's struggle against yielding to despair. We are not sure where Martha was in the stages of grief, but it was clear her brother was dead.

In this session's story we see Martha's struggle against yielding to despair. Her conversation with Jesus gives insight to the struggles we often face in believing that he is "the resurrection and the life."

READINGS

John 11:17-27, 38-44

17When Jesus arrived, he found that Lazarus had already been
in the tomb four days. 18Now Bethany was near Jerusalem,
some two miles away, 19and many of the Jews had come to
Martha and Mary to console them about their brother. 20When
Martha heard that Jesus was coming, she went and met him,
while Mary stayed at home.

21Martha said to Jesus, "Lord, if you had been here, my
brother would not have died. 22But even now I know that God
will give you whatever you ask of him."

23Jesus said to her, "Your brother will rise again."

24Martha said to him, "I know that he will rise again in the
resurrection on the last day."

25Jesus said to her, "I am the resurrection and the life.
Those who believe in me, even though they die, will live, 26and
everyone who lives and believes in me will never die. Do you
believe this?" 27She said to him, **"Yes, Lord, I believe that you
are the Messiah, the Son of God, the one coming into the
world."**

38Then Jesus, again greatly disturbed, came to the tomb. It
was a cave, and a stone was lying against it.

39Jesus said, "Take away the stone."

Martha, the sister of the dead man, said to him, "Lord,
already there is a stench because he has been dead for four
days."

40Jesus said to her, "Did I not tell you that if you believed,
you would see the glory of God?"

[41]So they took away the stone.

And Jesus looked upwards and said, "Father, I thank you for having heard me. [42]I knew that you always hear me, but I have said this for the sake of the crowd standing here, so that they may believe that you sent me."

[43]When he had said this, he cried with a loud voice, "Lazarus, come out!" [44]The dead man came out, his hands and feet bound with strips of cloth, and his face wrapped in a cloth. Jesus said to them, "Unbind him, and let him go."

DISCOVERING THE STORY

How is Martha dealing with her grief?

What are the barriers for Martha to trust Jesus?

In v. 21-22, is Martha doubting or affirming Jesus' abilities?

What does v. 24 reveal about Martha's faith at that point in the story?

What does Jesus mean when he says of himself, "I am the resurrection and the life?"

How does this expand Martha's understanding of him and deepen her trust in him?

What are the three "titles" she affirms about Jesus in v. 27?

DISCOVERING YOUR STORY

Has your faith ever been challenged by grief or a loss?

Compare how you reacted in a time of grief with Martha's faith, and the way she dealt with her brother's death.

When you hear the word "resurrection," what comes to mind?

_____ A past, one-time event
_____ A present experience of power
_____ A future hope
_____ A literal, historical event
_____ A metaphorical reference to a spiritual reality
_____ Other: ____________________

Think of ways to paraphrase: "I am the resurrection and the life."

What "titles" express what you believe about Jesus?

NOTES

For the context of the story, read John 11:1-44.

v. 17 — It was a common belief that the soul hovered over the body for three days in the hopes of reentering the body. The reference to four days made clear that Lazarus was dead.

v. 19 — For other references to Martha and Mary, see John 12:1-8 and Luke 10:38-42.

v. 21-22 — Compare Martha's statement with other expressions that combine faith and complaint in Psalms 4, 6, 13, and 22.

v. 24 – Compare this story's message with that of the Pharisees, who believed in the hope of a day of general resurrection at the end of time.

v. 25 – See other "I am" statements in John 6:35; 8:12; 10:7, 14 and 15:1.

Also see Yahweh's appearance to Moses in Exodus 3:13-15.

v. 27 – John uses formal confessional language to express Jesus' identity as the Messiah (his relationship with the Jews), and as the Son of God (his relationship with God). Compare with John 1:41, 49.

2. A Father's Story — From Anxiety to Assurance

INTRODUCTION

According to the Centers for Disease Control, about one in six children in the United States has a developmental disorder. The stress on parents is tremendous as they navigate the school system, seek services, and pay for medications.

This session's story describes a father whose son has very special needs.

Whether it is a child or an aging parent, a lonely neighbor, or a troubled coworker, nearly all of us find ourselves in the role of the caregiver at some point.

The burden of caring often takes a toll on our faith. Listen closely to this story about how a father hangs on to his faith in the face of an impossible situation, and finds assurance to keep on believing.

READING

Mark 9:14-29

14When [Jesus, Peter, James and John] came to the disciples, they saw a great crowd around them, and some scribes arguing with them. 15When the whole crowd saw him they were immediately overcome with awe, and they ran forward to greet him.

16He asked them, "What are you arguing about with them?"

17Someone from the crowd answered him, "Teacher, I brought you my son; he has a spirit that makes him unable to speak; 18and whenever it seizes him, it dashes him down; and he foams and grinds his teeth and becomes rigid; and I asked your disciples to cast it out, but they could not do so."

19He answered them, "You faithless generation, how much longer must I be among you? How much longer must I put up with you? Bring him to me."

20And they brought the boy to him. When the spirit saw him, immediately it convulsed the boy, and he fell on the ground and rolled about, foaming at the mouth.

21Jesus asked the father, "How long has this been happening to him?"

And he said, "From childhood. 22It has often cast him into the fire and into the water, to destroy him; but if you are able to do anything, have pity on us and help us."

23Jesus said to him, "If you are able! – All things can be done for the one who believes."

24Immediately the father of the child cried out, **"I believe; help my unbelief!"**

25When Jesus saw that a crowd came running together, he rebuked the unclean spirit, saying to it, "You spirit that keeps this boy from speaking and hearing, I command you, come out of him, and never enter him again!"

26 After crying out and convulsing him terribly, it came out, and the boy was like a corpse, so that most of them said, "He is dead."

27 But Jesus took him by the hand and lifted him up, and he was able to stand.

28 When he had entered the house, his disciples asked him privately, "Why could we not cast it out?"

29 He said to them, "This kind can come out only through prayer."

DISCOVERING THE STORY

What is wrong with the boy?

How do you think the father felt about his son's condition?

How do you think he felt about the inability of the disciples to heal him?

What does Jesus say to the crowd, and why does he say it?

Why does the father say, "I believe, help my unbelief?"

What made it difficult for the father to trust Jesus?

What does Jesus tell the disciples about the relationship between helping others and prayer?

DISCOVERING YOUR STORY

If you had been the father, what would you have said to Jesus?

Have you ever cared for someone with a chronic or long-term condition? What were the emotions you had to deal with?

Did the experience change your understanding of God?

Did it change your faith?

Have you ever gone through an experience during which you prayed, "I believe, help my unbelief?"

What spiritual practices have helped you as a caregiver?

NOTES

8:22-10:52 – Chapter 9 is part of a transitional section in Mark that features Jesus preparing the disciples for his upcoming and final ministry in Jerusalem. The disciples are being informed about his true identity, and about the deeper commitment required of them.

To illustrate this, Mark frames the section with two stories about healing the blind (8:22-26 and 10:46-52), and provides three predictions of Jesus' crucifixion and resurrection (8:31; 9:31 and 10:33-34). Just as the blind had their sight restored, so now the disciples will be able to see the real Jesus.

Part of this preparation is seeing a glimpse of the resurrected Messiah in the Transfiguration story that immediately precedes this story (9:2-13).

v. 14-29 – For comparison of this story in other gospels, see Matthew 17:14-21 and Luke 9:37-43.

v. 25 – The last references to exorcisms in Mark are found in chapter 9, here and in v.38-41. Most take place in the first part of the Gospel (See 1:21-26; 1:32; 3:11, 20-30; 6:3-6 and 5:1-20). Because the demon renders him mute, the boy cannot say the name of Jesus. The father is a proxy to express faith.

v. 28 – Contrast the disciples' inability to cast out the demon with 6:13.

v. 29 – A common Jewish assumption about miracles was that they were given in response to prayer. See 1:35 and 6:46 about Jesus praying alone.

3. A Mother's Story – From Exclusion to Inclusion

INTRODUCTION

The great African-American jazz singer Nina Simone sang in 1967:

I wish I could share
All the love that's in my heart
Remove all the bars
That keep us apart
I wish you could know
What it means to be me
Then you'd see and agree
That every man should be free.[1]

In this session's story, the Canaanite mother helps Jesus

know what it means to be her. It tested her faith and expands our vision of God's mercy.

READING

Matthew 15:21-28

21Jesus left that place and went away to the district of Tyre and
Sidon. 22Just then a Canaanite woman from that region came
out and started shouting, "Have mercy on me, Lord, Son of
David; my daughter is tormented by a demon."

23But he did not answer her at all.

And his disciples came and urged him, saying, "Send her away, for she keeps shouting after us."

24He answered, "I was sent only to the lost sheep of the house of Israel."

25But she came and knelt before him, saying, "Lord, help me."

26He answered, "It is not fair to take the children's food and throw it to the dogs."

27She said, **"Yes, Lord, yet even the dogs eat the crumbs that fall from their masters' tables."**

28Then Jesus answered her, "Woman, great is your faith! Let it be done for you as you wish."

And her daughter was healed instantly.

DISCOVERING THE STORY

What does her interaction with the Jewish rabbi and his disciples imply about the mother's status in society?

What did she think of Jesus?

How did she probably feel about his response (both his silence and his reply)?

What did Jesus mean in v. 24?

Are her words and actions an act of worship or a sign of subordination — or both?

What insights does she have about God's mercy in v. 27?

DISCOVERING YOUR STORY

Have you ever been an outsider?

When have you seen a church exclude someone?

Have you ever felt rejected or ignored by God?

Did it affect your ability to worship?

When has your understanding of God's mercy changed?

On a scale from one to five (one = not persistent; five = very persistent), how persistent and intentional are you in your relationships with the following:

_____ coworkers and supervisors
_____ family
_____ friends
_____ church
_____ God

NOTES

Chapter 13:53-16:12 — In this section, Jesus experiences opposition. The woman's faith is in sharp contrast to the lack of faith of his hometown neighbors (13:53-8), the disciples (14:22-36), and the Pharisees (16:1-12).

Besides the Pharisees demanding signs, Herod is also preoccupied with miracles (14:1-12), and Jesus tells John's disciples that his miracles are proof of his identity (11:2-6).

In contrast to Nazareth where Jesus was unable to perform many miracles due to the lack of faith of the residents, the Canaanite woman is exemplary.

For the parallel, see Mark 7:24-30. Mark calls her a Syrophoenician. The Greek word for woman (gynē) may indicate that she was a woman of high social status. Later in Christian tradition she is known as Justa and her daughter as Berenice in the Pseudo-Clementine homilies.

For comparison with her faith, see the story of the centurion in 8:5-13.

v. 21 — Tyre and Sidon: Jesus is in Gentile territory and outside of his realm of ministry as a Jewish Messiah. The region of Tyre was an ancient Phoenician city with a mixed population. There were several building projects by Herod the Great. According to Josephus, residents of Tyre were bitter enemies of the Jews, and at the outbreak of the Jewish War (66 c.e.) Tyrians killed and imprisoned many Jews. Jesus entered a hostile territory and is speaking to a woman who is part of a hostile people.

v. 26 — dogs: Not a household pet in Jewish culture; the

scene may presuppose a Gentile home as the setting (which is explicit in Mark's account).

4. Zacchaeus' Story — From Greed to Generosity

INTRODUCTION

We do not think of fundraising and religious conversion as two things that go together.

The spiritual writer Henri Nouwen disagrees: "Fundraising is always a call to conversion. And this call comes to both those who seek funds and those who have funds. Whether we are asking for money or giving money, we are drawn together by God, who is about to do a new thing through our collaboration.[2]"

It was a new thing that happened that day in Jericho when Jesus formed a collaboration with Zacchaeus. You may be familiar with the children's song: "Zacchaeus was a wee little man." The best part of the story comes after he gets down from the tree. Read what happens and discover the real change that took place in his faith.

READING

Luke 19:1-10

[1]He entered Jericho and was passing through it. [2]A man was there named Zacchaeus; he was a chief tax collector and was rich. [3]He was trying to see who Jesus was, but on account of the crowd he could not, because he was short in stature. [4]So he ran ahead and climbed a sycamore tree to see him, because he was going to pass that way.

[5]When Jesus came to the place, he looked up and said to him, "Zacchaeus, hurry and come down, for I must stay at your house today."

[6]So he hurried down and was happy to welcome him. [7]All who saw it began to grumble and said, "He has gone to be the guest of one who is a sinner."

[8]Zacchaeus stood there and said to the Lord, **"Look, half of my possessions, Lord, I will give to the poor; and if I have defrauded anyone of anything, I will pay back four times as much."**

[9]Then Jesus said to him, "Today salvation has come to this house, because he too is a son of Abraham. [10]For the Son of Man came to seek out and to save the lost."

DISCOVERING THE STORY

What kind of guy was Zacchaeus?

What did Zacchaeus desire in v.3?

Compare and contrast this desire with the desires of his occupation.

How are Jesus' words and actions an expression of generosity to Zacchaeus?

How did he feel about Jesus' reaction to him?

What does the crowd's reaction reveal about their assumptions about God's salvation?

In v. 8, what does Zacchaeus do, and why does he do it?

What does this story reveal about Jesus's mission?

DISCOVERING YOUR STORY

When have you been the recipient of generosity?

What is the link between hospitality and generosity?

When has your generosity been transformative of the recipient?

When has it transformed you as the giver?

When have you "gone out on a limb in your giving (either of time, emotional energy, or financial assistance)?

Did it change your faith?

What do you desire most?

Is this desire reflected in your relationship with money?

NOTES

Wealth – Issues of rich and poor play a prominent role in Luke's Gospel. In the Reign of God, there is a reversal of power between them (e.g. 1:46-55, 6:20-26). Greed and economic injustice are condemned (e.g. 11:42-44; 12:13-21, 16:19-31). The wise use of resources as a means for promoting God's realm is celebrated (e.g. 16:1-13, 19:11-27). Radical almsgiving is an expression of discipleship (e.g. 18:18-30, 21:1-4). These issues provide the context of 18:1-19:27 in which we read Zacchaeus' story.

v. 2 – Chief tax collector: Taxation was principally for the purpose of supporting the elite. There were imperial taxes and the temple tax. Often taxes were collected as tolls at booths which were staffed by collectors who were overseen by a chief tax collector. A chief tax collector was on contract with the Romans and had to pay in advance. Thus, the collector received a profit by charging more than what he had to pay, and thus the system was highly vulnerable to corruption.

v. 4 – Sycamore tree: The tree produced inferior figs which were only eaten by the poor.

v. 8 – Half my possessions...pay back four times; "defrauded" is the same verb used by John in his instructions to soldiers in 3:14; Exodus 22:1 refers to the repayment of fraud at this amount.

There were differences of interpretation regarding taxes

and fraud. By paying back at four times the original amount, Zacchaeus is opting for the most stringent interpretation of Jewish law.

v. 10 — Seek out: compare how the Son of Man seeks out Zacchaeus, who is seeking Jesus. The one seeking is being sought.

5. Your Story

INTRODUCTION

In this last session, you will write your faith story.

Jesus is not an ancient character in the Bible, but he meets each of us during our different journeys today. When we reflect on our stories, our faith grows. Our personal faith history becomes a point of reference to guide us through today's hardships and to tomorrow's hope.

STEP ONE

Review the previous sessions. Which character did you identify with?

_____ Martha
_____ the father
_____ the Canaanite mother
_____ Zacchaeus

Are there other people in the Bible you identify with?

Why do you identify with them?

STEP TWO

Looking back over the previous sessions, which key verse is the most meaningful for you?

Try to write a one-sentence statement that summarizes your faith.

STEP THREE

Plot your "spiritual timeline." Draw a line, and at the far left end write your birthdate, and at the right end write "today." Below the line put significant dates in your life, such as a graduation, wedding, divorce, a death, new job, and major illnesses.

Then, above the line, reflect back on those events in your life and record:

1.) the state of your faith at that time, and

2.) in looking back, what you think God was doing at that time.

STEP FOUR

The title of each session included the formula, "From _______ to _______."

Try writing this formula for yourself. Write your name and beside it fill in the blanks: "I came from __________ and I am going to _________."

STEP FIVE

The final step is to write your own spiritual autobiography. You may want to write it chronologically, using your timeline as an outline. You may want to write it as a poem or a song that highlights the key moments. You can use your favorite character as a comparison for yourself, or you can use your favorite verse as a title.

If writing is not your style, consider recording yourself.

For more on how to write your spiritual autobiography, read "The Story of Your Life: Writing Your Spiritual Autobiography" by Dan Wakefield.

---

[1] "Silk and Soul," RCA Records, 1967.

[2] "The Spirituality of Fundraising," Nashville: Upper Room Books, 2010, p. 17.

About the Author

Darren Cushman Wood is the senior pastor of North United Methodist Church in Indianapolis, Indiana. He has served small and large, rural and urban United Methodist churches for over 30 years. He is a graduate of the University of Evansville and Union Theological Seminary.

He is the author of two books, hymns, and numerous articles. He is an adjunct professor of labor studies at Indiana University. He is married to Ginny and as of this writing they have three adult children and one grandchild.

www.ingramcontent.com/pod-product-compliance
Lightning Source LLC
LaVergne TN
LVHW020313110826
845148LV00017BA/2654
* 9 7 9 8 9 8 8 2 3 3 2 0 6 *